A

A Rage of Love

Translated from the Italian
by Pasquale Verdicchio

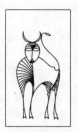

Guernica
Toronto / New York
1996

Original Title:

Delirio amoroso

The original work was published by Melangolo editore in 1989.

Copyright © Melangolo editore, 1989.

Translation © Pasquale Verdicchio and Guernica Editions Inc., 1996.

All rights reserved.

The translator wishes to thank Fanny How for her help.

Antonio D'Alfonso, Editor.

Guernica Editions Inc.

P. O. Box 117, Station P, Toronto (Ontario), Canada M5S 2S6

340 Nagel Drive, Cheektowaga, N.Y. 14225-4731 U.S.A.

Typesetting by Jean Yves Collette.

Printed in Canada.

This publication was assisted by the Minister of Foreign Affairs (Government of Italy)
through the Istituto Italiano di Cultura in Toronto (Director: Francesca Valente)
and Vancouver (Director: Gabriella Bianco).

Legal Deposit – First Quarter.

National Library of Canada.

Library of Congress Catalog Card Number: 93-81344.

Canadian Cataloguing in Publication

Merini, Alda, 1931- .

A rage of love

(Prose series ; 30)

Translation of: Delirio amoroso.

ISBN 1-55071-013-3

I. Title II. Series.

PQ4873.E74Z46413 1995 858'.91407 C94-900794-3

96 97 98 99 10 9 8 7 6 5 4 3 2 1

A Rage of Love

1

My greatest wish is to have an ambulance waiting, just like Salvador Dali. It happened once when I was thirty-four when, after having read a horoscope that predicted a fun outing, I found myself in the grip of four male nurses who threw me into a Green Cross van. They were all very gracious and joyful. They kept patting me on the back, I was proud: four strapping young men reassuring me and giving me all their attention.

"Finally," I said, opening the window, "some fresh air."

"Of course, of course," said one nurse, "air of open weeping."

I was unloaded at the entrance of the Paolo Pini Institute, but I had still not understood. Blessed spirits don't believe that there is violence in the world. So I stayed in that tormentuous and foul place that is an insane asylum. God, what awful words! Lost, I searched for the four young men who had flown and instead I found a man out of his wits who slapped me hard and said: "This is only the beginning" – and then left with a bothered air.

When the curtain is dropped in a theatre, sometimes the marionettes are out, extinguished. We look in vain for nightingales of love. In vain we look for the shards of rosaries. Our father was analyzed without psychoanalysis. Get rid of the psychiatric clinics that protect us from wildness! Delirium is so large!

Oh, cruel women, women who have never felt pain and don't know what it means. Women who use their children as a mirror, be careful not to let your betrayal be reflected within it. You, who understand work as that which is purely manual or pedagogic. There is a subtle love that you have never tried: it is God's hard pressure that works on me and at times causes me to bleed.

This pressure worked in my mind and this maybe was my major undoing, beyond my physical and mental torments. Or maybe it was this pain, higher than all others, that saved me. Saturated as I was, with true biblical pain, I did not think to cover my shoulders, and became so bold and open as to seem to invite the attention of would-be lovers.

Today I am still the same: a woman who perspires love and suffering. A woman who perspires sentiments of shame and tenderness. Any hint of suffering arouses men's desires for me. And what does not provoke a man's lust! His sadism in fact matures at the sight of destroyed flesh. Though neither beautiful nor inviting, flesh full of ire and suffering generates lust. Forgive me then for the extreme comparison. Is there anything more amoral than an insane asylum? The shame of the nakedness offered as sacrifice was God's shame as well. It was maybe at this point, my God, that you and I cried.

My mother, looking at me, said: "You have well set hips. You will be fertile."

Sure, fertile, a fertile soil in which to plant. But I also had a spirit and maybe my mother had not noticed it. I was delicate, shy and my prodigious body bothered me. I would stand apart, asking myself if my poetry was equal to my body and my body equal to my poetry. I wanted to be diaphanous, sweet and pale. Maybe that's where the trap was set.

I am a being frustrated by dementia.

The dementia emerged suddenly, one day, when my mother, with the birth of my brother, said: "Put away your books. You can't study any longer: the boy is born."

In those days boys were sacred. The male had to contain all the moral and physical reserves of the family and of its immediate environment. I was a student, in my first year of medicine. I wanted a degree. A degree for me meant a desk, a respectable position, a ready smile for each new client. I wanted to be a doctor. When he said that from pain a sound is born, he was right. An obsession was born. And the obsession became poetry. Beautiful, hendecasyllabic, because playing music had also been forbidden me. The mental atonality caused by the absence of music is quite formidable. Beyond the missing scalpel, the missing medicine, I also missed my adored piano.

And so I got back to my lot. Going to work in Via Verdi, walking in front of the Garzanti publisher's bookstore, I, an adolescent, used to think: "One of my books, there in the window, I wonder when!" I had to wait thirty-five years, thirty-five. I used to go hide out in Via del Torchio. Maybe I became a poet because I didn't care much for poetry. Even if I read book after book, even if song was in me (but it was the song of life, and this they did not understand). To be a woman of letters did not mean that I should be unwomanly, I even wanted to be a good mother.

In Via del Torchio I had contact with my first poetic community. By community I mean that I sat on the same couch, elbow to elbow, with the greats of poetry. In the class of literary innovation. I was too young to understand what those great men were doing.

Luciano Erba, always happy and dispersive. Pasolini, quiet but always full of physical resistance. Turoldo, with a beautiful and thundering voice that seemed the reincarnation of a redeemed *scapigliatura*.

We were poor, but full of patience and attentive. I was not a writer, to them I was a mascot: young, quiet, maybe beautiful, with two hips that embarrassed me and I tried to hide.

Giorgio Manganelli was good natured. He would dribble his food down the front of my dress and laugh, but it was a tender laugh. Erba always looked as if he was seeking a kite that had flown from his hands.

Schwarz, at a certain point, proposed the publication of my first book: *The Presence of Orpheus*.

Everyone invited me out and I always declined. I was very attached to my family. Many wanted to marry me. I opted for three doctors at the same time and married none. And when I decided to enter a convent, I thought I had made a good choice.

We all trafficked in spiritual goods. But the intellectuals would hide behind large volumes only in order to stare at the skirts of beautiful women.

Thinking again about the time passed in Via del Torchio, I should say that, yes, those were serene times, but not totally, since I was searching for poetry, searching for truth.

Culturally content, I wrote *The Presence of Orpheus*. *The Presence of Orpheus* is the lament of the soul that finds itself in the hydric hell of the body. It is unable to leave the darkness. The soul that breaks out is inexplicably caught in Pluto's jaws. I am still in the mouth of that miserable dog. I have called this dog mafia. The mafia is the subtrefuge of earthly jealousy that comes upon me without warning, that has interrupted the musical sound of my shadows.

At nine the gadget goes off. If I don't go to the psychiatrist anxiety begins to eat me up and my soul dies. And so I go in to be revitalized, but in order to do this I place the future of my body in serious danger, and it scares me. Two fears cannot co-exist, and I tremble with shame.

Often people ask what poetry yields in the way of a reward. Money wise I don't think it yields anything, but at the physical level it keeps my bowels regular. This odd connection, rather than upsetting me, angers me. Since the beginning, since the time of my development, this curse has persecuted me: such a violent body, generous and conflicted, and a soul of milk and honey. I understand that these things don't belong together. When this balance is disturbed psychiatry comes into play. In order to make that prodigious machine work, the body-soul of the poet, it must be taken in to the psychiatrist.

Even the mentally ill have a certain attractive quality. The mentally ill are slippery like mud, like quicksand. They move inside it; and the illness is a whirlpool that takes a hold of you and often does not return you to life.

This woman who wants neither to die nor to be suppressed after intercourse is the new woman of our times. Rather than give birth to the word she pronounces it. The woman poet who does justice in the name of her own voice and who figuratively represents the language has her own figure: she has centralized and given life to these cultural signs.

Being insane myself, I distrust the insane. If I were to let them take advantage of me imagine then what those who are not mentally ill would do, with their guards and discipline and clinical charts. And so, for a long time, I did not trust Dino Campana, telling myself that after all his *Orphean Cantos* were only one of his peripheric dimensions and that the author's central reality consisted in his folly. For the mentally ill, folly is the center of life. They are always involved in the struggle against their own shadows. Yes, of course, Campana was distracted by his own interests. My eye fell upon a passage where he mentions the benevolence of social workers: I don't agree with him. First of all, those women should never go near a poet. When they encounter a poet they dismember him, they study him carefully, they evaluate and put a price on him. But, above all, they make a medical diagnosis as a caution. Campana pampered by the ladies of San Vincenzo really scares me. It's there that he becomes dangerous: when he enters the sources of illness that are as acute and terrible as bourgeois righteousness. I too, like him, have been manipulated by them, by the careful and smug air of "good people." In fact, these people have only one thing on their mind: their own well-being. That their own time, even that of their bowel movements, not be disturbed. They are the ones who belong in the insane asylum, even before the doctors.

If art is hard, pass alongside it in silence. You won't find a man at the end of it waiting for you. Nor will you find an olive branch. If art is deep like your mother, listen to her in silence: that is where you die.

It's my perennial religion that forces me to live, not my poetry: that sweet young woman has by now disappeared in the secrets of my memory. But when does memory have secrets? When it forgets.

I live in the clearing of the soul. I no longer have secrets.

Castles of my silences, castles of my pain, times of obscure marvels. Outside they sing songs about the ruthless night. And you flourish inside those bitter and deaf herbs of my memory. Why did you hurt me? I had lived in a prison, and you made me a prisoner once more with your song of love.

And so I dedicate a song to you, and inside this song your question is like a fist, when you asked me: "How did you move from truth to folly?" I don't know, I don't want to know, it's so wonderful to be lost.

There are souls so light and numismatic that they are like sphinxes. At times, one falls asleep and slowly loses one's soul. The soul is that hidden thing that tastes of sweat, that oppresses and compresses and that doesn't usually cheer up. It twists and despairs.

I'd like to hear someone who is happy with their soul, someone say so. But who could be happy with an absent body? At times the soul turns itself upside down and presents a tremendous backside.

When the soul brays, it does so clamorously and it is not reconcilable with the mass of the body. And since the soul brays in spite of the body, a strange symbiosis with psychoanalysis develops.

The injurious weeping of mental illness is not an authentic weeping, it's a useless weeping.

Often I think about entering a convent, but one cannot be faithful because of disappointments with the world. God is not an alternative to earthly love. God must be a choice, a hint of music, like on a piano. When God touches you, it can be horrific because it is scary as well. When I was in the asylum, and used to see grass from the side of its roots, I was convinced (and I still am) that the great fabric, the great canopy of divine will is visible to the angels. We, who are on the path of indolence or extreme sacrifice, understand nothing. The difficulty comes in accepting the fact that dishonourable and unscrupulous people make choices for you that only God should make. This great question (if it is legitimate to act apart from

God) makes me furious toward man. For this great and useless question I have been punished. But I absolve myself of this.

When I am very sad I cry. I have built a dream house above the lake of the Gethsemane. Why there? Because I adore my religion and my Christ.

In that tranquil place I have built a sweet hut outfitted with air and honey. I go there to live with Him. We lie softly on the hard ground and dream together. It's beautiful to dream the same dreams, those dreams that only the pariahs and the distant dream. Dreams both weak and strong like the souls of children. We are naked because clothes cannot cover us: we are good and are appreciated by the angels.

There exist some ancient necklaces known as "the necklaces of the Prophets" and they are nothing more than Samson's hair, which give man strength when he empathises with nature.

They are beautiful to see; no one has seen them, but they are known to exist.

All of chiromanzy is continually searching for the place where they may be buried. These necklaces are talismans, and do not lay on the earth but in the air and are almost invisible to the naked eye. At times one feels a fluttering as if something had passed near, one feels strangely exalted. The loved one returns, and the rose finally opens. You begin to marvel at the world because these necklaces that pass through the air have grazed you. You even begin to bless others, and become benevolently insane, like Saint Francis. The negromants, and the cartomants, who do not know what they are, will never find them, because these wandering necklaces are the wings of angels.

Christ did not want a funeral. Think of what contemporary undertakers would say: Christ left in silence so as not to give them his money, after having made such a spectacle of himself. This is just and sacrosanct. Of course I say this with no intention of insulting the Church. Mine are but the ridiculous dribblings of an awkward writer.

To think that Christ never wanted a savings account either gives me much pleasure. It means, in effect, that not only was He the son of God but was also a great socialist.

The Son of God must have been romantic, languid, stupendous, beautiful. But what in the devil am I saying! God and the devil don't ever agree. And how could I "tempt" this antichrist? ...But didn't He have other things to do? Why didn't the devil ruin Him in forty days of fasting? ...What a confusion of people, of sexes, of abstractions ...The Christ emerges, yes, but Christ is maternal, and that scares me: His wide open arms and His chest without breasts...

One day I had a vision of a God that was falling heavily from the cross, while something told me that it was the hour of some horrible artistic and spiritual clock. It was as if a violent repossessor of Paradise had entered the Eden of my love.

Something similar had to have happened at the beginning of creation, when Lucifer dominated over Satan.

The Catholic religion, so full of paradox, is able to ruin even the intimate interests of man, and his search for God. God is freedom, and not dishonor. God forgives. Only men are the eternal inquisitors. Maybe that's why feminism was born. It true that woman has a body overall similar to man's and that she must have the freedom to love and not only obey the desires of men. With this I don't mean to say that man is equal to woman and viceversa.

But no one must compare themselves with God, but rather remember that God is all forgiving with those who have sinned or transgressed. In truth this is a diary made of empty guilt. I have alway had enough judgement to know that some conditions are to be respected. For this reason I called his ten sons "the ten commandments." Because their judgement damned my soul. At one time I thought I might have been preyed upon by demons, but it wasn't true. I think that actually the demon ignored a fool overburdened with Catholic poison. Very foolish because God is absolute liberty.

I have been betrayed: I don't know by whom. One day a gray cloud fell upon my existence. A colourless cloud. It's difficult for men to move the skies, and at times they make use of fortune-tellers for such a task. With cauldrons, with snakes and witches I was sent far from my homeland to where I knew of nothing. I was buried in psychiatry. Because of honor, because of power. The "diary" became my passport to a folly dense with love and poverty. I am poor, only the alms of friends allow me to live on. There is romanticism in this, but I remain fundamentally poor. I would like to have my secret dominion. If I am betrayed, I hide in the knotted mass of words and words are green and tall hedges where the honest hares squat.

Man is a cannibal that must absolutely eat his own, after which he clamorously displays his electronic machinery, his latest model washers, his computers and everything else he calls progress (and which I call massacre).

Schizophrenia is the fatal schism of two who are the same subject. I was held in isolation for fifteen days, which brought about a terrible nervous collapse, along with fear. And fear is in the human soul like a desert. And so began the process of decay and retreat of my poetic personality. Then I dissolved into many small fragments very difficult to reunite except through analysis. When the *I* breaks apart it is like the presence of a man, a negative form of man. This is the initial trauma. It is the figure of an aggressor who comes to twist at the groin of poetic power. In this way my great unbalance began, and the inability to reunite myself. I found, for a second time, the system of asylums. Highly negative, useless and destructive.

My schizophrenia, so acclaimed by the critics, was nothing more than the epilogue of a funereal story, an evil shadow of a childhood tragedy. A memory not visible, and then expressed as a prayer of liberation, in long poetic lamentations. Analysis was helpful in focusing in on this atmophere of desire and guilt and finally it gave me a semblance of an existence.

The embezzlement, the intrigues, the compromises that the operators of the Psychiatric Centers resort to are incredible in order to trap the patient that speaks, discusses, denounces. The patient is guilty: all of this is, for them, psychiatric knowledge. All of this is for me a crime.

I am at odds with four terrible psychiatrists. The trial has begun.

Let me tell you of what it consists: there is an internal tribunal on which the "friend" psychiatrist who imposes her law invariably sits. The others appraise her suppositions. On the left, there sits a woman psychologist with glasses, upheld by a dependable psychologist. On the right, we have the universal director of the C.P.S. Further down, there are four nurses. The law comes from the psychiatrist friend, who is always punctual with her appointments. Every day you climb up on the cross. They keep you there for a few hours, they bear witness, they dress you well, they feed you myrrh orally, but they almost always make mistakes. The three kings never appear. The resurrection does not take place. The trial has no divine laws, not even human ones. It's a closed door trial and it comes under the dominion of psychiatry.

You say you want love. "What type?" asks the doctor.

"Of the most convenient type" you answer. "Well, to tell the truth, of the most absolute type possible."

"The spirit does not exist," the woman psychologist intervenes, "right, nurse?"

"Yes, in fact the spirit does not exist, therefore you are delirious."

The five heads nod in agreement. You hazard: "What should I do?"

"Get fucked!" shouts a patient from backstage, but he is quickly subdued.

"Well, as I was saying, you have a love fixation. Contemplated sentiments are not considered by our psychiatry. Is that alright with you?"

"Of course," you say with fear and disdain.

"Good, here let's move into normalcy, or else things are going to take a bad turn."

At times, I would flounder about on the floor. Like a strange snake eating its own guts. In front of an empty television set, crying: "God, do me justice!"

But I never understood what type of justice I wanted, because I AM the only person who will not pardon me.

2

He wanted to repay me for my many years of suffering. I already loved him. One day he called me on the phone, maybe someone had suggested it, maybe he was sincerely impressed: this is an unpenetrable point in our story. In time his words became more and more fiery, I ended up in flames, eventually giving vent to the impulses of love I had held in for years, first because of the asylum, then due to the death of my husband.

I was born destined to suffer. I wished my own death. But life was ferocious: it let me survive. When my husband died, and I received a sum of money from the University of Pavia, still full of pain and love for that great poet, I left for the city of Taranto.

I had thought of the South as a backward land: I had shaped this idea by watching the poor southerners of the Naviglio. But Taranto was full of song, melody and sun. And then there he was: beautiful, tall, austere, silent and threatening. But I did not fear him. Poets are never afraid of each other, because they know that beneath their strength there is a vulnerability as deep as the ocean.

He wanted to help me and recompense me for those horrible years. He sensed how hard and alienating they were. And also he noticed the faith by which I had lived through them in the darkness of insanity. As I've already said, the *Diary*, written twenty years later, is not a true depiction since the horrors have been removed and forgotten. Everyone, after having lived through a terrible period in their lives, and having overcome it, tends to forget the evil suffered and received. It's a little like giving birth, a wonderful physiological process: if all mothers remembered what they suffered during labour there would be no more children. In fact, nature is quite a provider and erases the worst moment.

He was very discrete. When he suffered he did not let on: he had an excessive sense of pudor. I complained to him about this: of wanting to take care of himself at all costs, without my help. He felt inferior to me sexually, and this made him sad. He accompanied me everywhere to prove to himself that he was still young. This effort on his part made me happy, because I knew that it would help him write his best poetry: no poetry exists without enormous physical effort. Just the same, this physical effort might also undermine his health, as it had done with mine. Poetry is not only a mission: it is also, and above all, manual labour. Only by drawing close to natural forces is it possible to arrive at contemplation.

Entering his family I entered a noble household where guilt is absent and becomes, if anything, superstition. Familial canons dominate like a wooden scalpel over human will. I was in the place of idols. In the ancestral place where passions are accepted, lived and dreamed. One day I read him a love poem where the man was sixty and the woman thirty. He liked it very much. We loved his children. I, who had never been able to live with my own, hoped that finally this could be my family. I adored those beautiful children and secretly thanked their mother, who had created them so strong and united.

He was a great poet. He would disappear into his studio where he would stay for hours, in silence. Afterward he would come into my room to read me his poems, asking my opinion: those years lived in medicine had installed crudeness and hermeticism in his language but still he spoke a great poetry.

I loved him. We loved each other very much and both lived in peace. But one day, as if by the hand of a pedantic surgeon, or as if by some well paid witch who turned good into evil, someone decided to cure this infection of love.

It might be said that my life has been a constellation of damnations. If it's true that the stars affect our existence, then an evil star governed my life.

He was not handsome, but he had the beauty of a far seeing sage. At times he would sit beside me, in the warm evening, and would begin to talk. Our bed was ancient, uncared for over time. "In this bed," he used to say, "my children were born."

I never changed the position of, or modernized, that bed. I made no changes to that house: I knew how much he cared for his things.

He would tell me about C., the magpie that untied his shoelaces and stole pieces of glass in order to take them to its hidden nest. "You know," he would say, "they killed it." I could understand how that bird could mean nothing to anyone but for him it represented a part of his soul, that stole reality in order to hide it away in myth.

The most wonderful hours were those that we passed in complete solitude, stretched out on the bed, hand in hand. He would bitterly tell me of things past, but he never judged others. When I chanced an hypothesis that someone could harm us, he would say: "Quiet, God knows all our mysteries."

It bothered me when he talked about his guilt: I could not find any sin in him.

I had heard it said that as a youth he had been astonishingly bold.

Sometimes we would go to the ocean. In front of that enormous expanse I would say to him: "Try to imagine all the submerged wonders, and how many things engender and destroy each other in the bowels of the sea." He would answer: "I was born near the ocean, but now I feel as if I have always been from Milano; the sea no longer interests me."

Meanwhile, the scirocco, like a warm and dulling hand, would become overpowering and life would flow in slow motion: it was like a dreary film, at times summarily lively, but always a little sinister.

But that high sun of Taranto was able to infiltrate below the eyelids and recall a life by then dispossessed. That indecent and deep sun, that gulf open to any possible expansion of love! It was beautiful and large, and shining over the love I had for him. When together we reached the presence of God, we disintegrated into poetry. We would sit like kings at the caffè table. Everyone would look at us. Maybe they suspected me of being a mercenary woman: in the south this is what they think of northern women.

In the South, weather changes with little warning. An intense coldness would change to an epidemic and voluptuous heat and create certain physiological and environmental mutations. I was particularly not well disposed to such changes. I am a woman who loves continuity, particularly the continuity of sensations. Those internal and external changes (from meteoropatia) made me impatient. I would have liked to leave his house, but much more I would have liked to leave myself, change skin. It was a time of strange discoveries: all at once, I'd understand that an underground crack had opened up within myself, and at times it released poisonous and sulphurous gases. Hell was at hand. Both hell and the knowledge of God. And of the *I*. Meeting the *I* is like doubling in a play with death. In the South I had met my double, and it could have been him, but it was also a sentimental call of which I knew neither the source nor its death. An almost diabolical dimension of knowledge, uterine one might say, that I found difficult to express or discuss. His patience and skill helped me very much. Afterall, by marrying him I had placed into question my whole existence.

Maybe we were never happy, or maybe we were too happy. It hovered above us like an imprecise shadow, the shadow of an unadmitted guilt, the shadow that enslaves men. He used to repeat: "We are like two Renzo chickens, tied to the same string. I wonder who will slap us down on the table without pity." The cord was that of poetry. The table, our human substance. Over our bed ran a terrifying fault, reminder of a past Taranto earthquake. They had left it as it was because it was reminiscent of the horror of a invisible time. That crack seemed to bring back an epoch.

He would rise at dawn, go through his papers, and disappear into his study. I was calm. I had completed the cycle of my life, I had written the *Diary*.

When we came to Milano, he was happy like a child. We would reserve a sleeping compartment and would lock ourselves in, dreamy and longing for love. What happy times they were. And those were long, interminable voyages of vacation. I would usually sleep in the top bunk, so that he could comfortably get out of his bed. He was middle-aged, and every time he woke up he would give a little smile, as if to say "Sorry to disturb you." He kept an eye on his jacket hanging on the wall. He would never look at himself in the mirror; usually, I would comb his hair. The few hair left on his almost completely bald head filled me with infinite tenderness. I thought of how much that soul might have suffered in his slow and arduous mission as doctor. He would boldly show me his hand with the wedding band and would say: "No one will ever take this from us." But, in fact, it was taken from both of us. And we were divided, our souls torn from each other, with one dangerous blow.

He was able to see me as young through his love and his poet's conformation. He called me "daddy's treasure." At times, he was lovable; at others, he was grumpy: I could not imagine his being ill. He who held himself up like a soldier. Ours was a model marriage, a marriage of love, of true love. Then one day he became fixated: he wanted to have the operation. It was a mistake. He wanted to be my husband at all levels, it still pains me that he had not yet understood how for me he was in any case the man of my dreams. In the South men take pride in their virility. We pay less attention to it, our husbands also become our sons. But he had taken the role of the father and very loving husband but always in command. It's hard for a poet to let himself be dominated by someone. Maybe we should have accepted each other with our weaknesses and our sense of supremacy: we were two strong spirits, so strong as to challenge the entire universe.

He was full of himself, I was thirsty for discovery: he did not include me in his science (or maybe he was simply tired). But every day in the tabernacle of his library, in his study, he forgave himself. At times, I asked myself what might have had a hold of him: what suspicion, what guilt, what undecipherable mystery of the soul could turn him upside down when he lost his omnipotence as a father. He had ten children who knew of their father's possession of the knowledge and the secrets of life.

"The Closed Door" was the one they again closed behind me after they had separated me from him. From then on that door was closed forever, because following the operation he remained in a state of unconsciousness, maybe in a demented state.

I did not want him to go to church in order to relieve his guilt. His had become a religion that asphixiated him. "I am your companion now, and God is with us," but he continued with his unhappy monologue that delighted him, like Saint Francis found delight in his poverty.

I said that is was useless to blame anyone or anything. He thought so too. He believed destiny to be the only creator. Following that, my doctor told me that the best cure is life. But life is not willing to cure me, therefore it can only kill me.

All of us at the Centre are ill with life, we are nostalgic. The lack of money, love, sex, those are all pretexts. Life is what is lacking. This evening, during a radio program, a Father said: "Christ was the great sexual liberator." And so, Christ has liberated sex. He gave it a human dimension, not esoteric. To love Him, with all the passion of my fifty years was already great Christianity. Only the hard mischiveous ones saw it otherwise. It was the great Christianity of the Madeleine, of Saint Augustine, of Saint Francis and of all the Saints who have loved and who cannot justify spiritual death when the pain that sustains it is lacking. To love Him meant to desire Him. To love Christ means to ingest His body: He who has suffered sex and has surpassed it. To resemble Christ means to surpass this miserable, earthly, human dimension, that is undeniably also love. A dimension that has been lived and violated by the sanctity of Jesus.

In other minds sex came to mean vice. There was talk of sexual block (and so they spoke of it in psychiatry). I, instead, speak of a blockage of love, which, not finding its harmony, no longer wants to love life.

Sure, he was not perfect, and this pleased me. It gave me pleasure to know that above all I had married a human being. I never believed in achieving status. Culture should only marvel those who acquire it. He held an enormous amount of knowledge which he held in silence, almost always shy about expressing it. I reproached him about this.

They have separated me from my love in a most ignoble manner. The field workers of thought. We loved each other very much. We were two free poets, free through all time, through every season. We loved each other outside of our senses and beyond them. Despite this our love had all the signs of passion.

In the South, something ancient and mysterious, a warm memory of the dead, makes everything previously touched sacred. One could carry out some study on *amorous dementia* and difficult and foul ancestral pathos. He too was catalogued among the dead while still living. But he was a simple man, a simple man who could not believe in his children's meanness; in the same way that I still today cannot believe in the indifference of my children, even after two years of the most absolute desolation.

If my daughter had come to take me away from the ward in Taranto, when I was undone by fear and by internal illness, I would not have had to suffer through that harsh, dolorous calvary of solitude. Today too. Every day is a cleansing of mental hygene. And even if it is true that my doctor helped me out of that terrible gulf of pain and ignominy that is the Taranto ward, it is also true that afterward my recovery was so slow, difficult and painful as to carry me over to a second madness.

If I knew he were dead, I would cover myself with ashes. But I am always hopeful that he will take shelter here, and meanwhile I damn fate, because I know that he is not alive. But my reason has not altogether given up, and so, in the tangle of my weeping, I hold the image of my great one alive. Oh my children, if I were to understand that he is dead I would lose my mind altogether while, when I warm myself with madness, I do not let go. And this is my suffering.

What I have endured in these two years of total isolation, during which I stayed in the most modern and luxurious psychiatric ward of the soul, lamenting my destroyed love! I consider my works, so poorly paid that I have picked up the pen again. Such physical and terrible pain that I have to call the internist every now and then. The good doctor R. also came by, but maybe no one had faith in my poor body annihilated by the poisonous effects of love. When love is suddenly eliminated, it vents itself on its subject with incurable and bewitching violence.

My home and my existence with the man I loved was gone. I denied the life that had allowed death to enter his body. I even denied him, for having allowed it. And this was my fatal abstraction. My own madness pushed me to the annihilation of my own life.

The impact of reality and life produces a cruel love, constant and benumbed by the cold. He is the one that emerges from the shadows. He wants silence, and it is He who wants the delirium.

How could I not construct for Him a serene but unacceptable arc of madness?

The psychiatrist wants to destroy me, wants to destroy the body of Eros, and Eros has the magnificent wings of the religious praying mantis. Now, in the memory of Him, religion has become damnation. Christ HAS become abominable. And He is not dead, because if He were, I would stop writing. And by ceasing to write I would no longer argue with those who want to chase me down. The great Greek mythology through which Sappho sang her solitude and her desire for love is defeated and in the violence of the ten tentacles of love I am defeated, once again defeated.

There exist forms of illness and of love so enveloping as to recall the prehensile tentacles of a squid. That is why I spoke of fear. Fear is in our souls. It is as if a concert of witches and mnemonic rites were able to produce a miracle, or a destructive circuit of thought.

I had fallen in love, but in a manner so destructive and total as to lose my identity. And when they took him from me I lost the principle of my love as well, which means, virtually, I lost the reason for life. I did not know who to blame for this, and I was myself already saturated with guilt that I could not have carried more weight. And so I wandered, almost stupidly, into the psychiatric ward of Taranto.

I did not know that after the Basaglia Law insane asylums were still in function: in the South there existed a fully functioning one. I had written *Diary*, which represented a battle against the abuses of psychiatry in Milano, against the abuses of the rights of the ill. Delirium is freedom taken to its extreme frustration. In delirium the patient becomes a child and becomes, above all, alien in the sense that he comes into contact with other spiritual freedoms. When they tell me that I am a witch, I laugh. Witches are a medieval concept. Rather, we should talk about pain as an initiation, because pain is an extrordinary initiation to all types of knowledge. The hospital in Affori had been a good school. Even now that it has closed down it continues to live on in the minds of those who were there.

The mentally ill suffer unnameable persecutions, no one knows why. They assume the role of saint in today's society, since it is presumed that they, rarefied by their own madness, do not suffer like everyone else. If only the outsiders knew of what goes on in the poor mind of the sick, what mischiefs and tricks mental illness carries out! Totally unaware of illness like this, people consider shopping, taking care of the house, and fucking to be of primary importance.

His death translates the death of the soul. He was my love, my hope of similar resurrection. He was the one to give the title *The Other Truth* to my *Diary of a Different Woman*. He understood that the truth of the ill is an unequivocal reality. What horrible things happened in that psychiatric ward I don't know. I know that I went there spontaneously, almost guided by an adverse destiny. I was dragged there, I remember, by something. As if by a precise instance. The instance of the end of a verse that obliges one to go to the beginning of the next had translated me into that horrible ward. I had fallen ill exactly at the same time he started to become ill: I could not accept that a second death would force itself on me.

He always suffered. From the closed door of my room I could hear his tormented screams. I could not intervene directly and I hardly knew the doctors that were tending to him. I knew for certain, though, that being a doctor himself, he could not mistake his own diagnosis. But he did not communicate it to me, and this not knowing what was happening to him, this faith in me, exasperated me day after day.

When they shut that door, in Taranto, they also closed the door on my reason, and for a long time after I could not pick up a pen. *The Closed Door* will be the title of my next novel.

And I am alive, after these two years of pain, and he is dead.

Down there, in the ward in Taranto, the doctors whispered: "She doesn't seem to understand that she'll never see him again." And I looked for him, looked for him everywhere, dragging myself across the floor, screaming as if from strong birthing pains and saying: "God, do me justice." The brothers helped me. One Father said: "Don't be like the woman who was frightened as she looked on the Nativity Scene. Go on, you too can conceive."

These dear monks, so fervid, happy and full of opinions. But the door, the door of dementia, was still closed.

I refuse to believe that he is dead, I will search for him. I am ill, but I will not cure myself, because he is my only doctor.

One day escaping from the ward in Taranto I went to the windows of his apartment. I called out to him. I heard his daughter say, "Father, you cannot cure her, you too are ill, she will forget."

I went back to shut myself in the ward with a broken heart. Even Rocco, the porter, seeing me, lowered his head.

At thirty one dies from love. At sixty from waiting. No age has a true "triumph." But maybe, by never asking for anything, one can arm oneself with a word and it is then that the imprecise arch of vengence begins.

When I lost him, I was not even called to his funeral. They always believed that I had married him out of some other interest, but it was not so. I loved him, and it was only natural that he had thought about my future.

I will search for him along naked paths. I will search for him beyond death, beyond the lost paradise. I know where he lives: he has entered into a symbiosis with my mind. Two different minds become one mind in madness.

To return to the Naviglio after a four year absence was more than painful for me, it was inhuman. To be uprooted from one's environment, not be able to find roots, country, nor a bed of love. That bed of quiet desire, the bed of births, in Taranto, was thrown out (as a euphemism) and so I returned to mine, which had become a psychiatric bed. The bandages that wrap me are terrible and painful, and for two years I escaped only so that I may return there.

The Naviglio, tired, turbulent, difficult, ancient, overburdened, guilty, whorish, drugged by dreams, re-touched by the knowing hand of consumerism, today looks like a joyful prancing prostitute. Instead, I remember the naked rocks, the paradoxical moments of folly, the swearing, the cigarette butts left by those who washed their clothes there, my children that languished with hunger, the ambulances that would take me away and then bring me back, depending on their moods. My troubled pupils, my piano. The free songs, the hosannas of the demons. The table empty of friendships and the anxiety of a mother who was about to leave for a hermit-age and was fully aware of it. All that love and solitude! What spare anguish in that phallic divination that not even the church could undo! The Naviglio, flowing like a tear. My face, a large tear on the Naviglio.

People recognized me when I returned, carefully watched and mocked me, offended, shunned, and reaccepted me. I had to beg forgiveness of every woman of business, every clothes washer, every host, for being a poet.

How many times I returned to this house with a branch of peace in my mouth. And that branch was given me at the door of the insane asylum along with the dove that carried it there. A dove with a belly full of love and desire to regenerate. Regenerate *ad infinitum,* but well aware that its eggs could be cracked by an enemy hand.

Then, one day, the surf of Taranto threw onto the white shores of the Naviglio an almost dead body. No one gathered me up. Someone kicked me in the ribs and my heart hurt: a tremendous bruise that penalized the solar plexus. And so, doubly weighed by spaces and memories, I opened a gate. It should have been the gate of a building; in reality, it was that of the new, secret poetic psychiatry. In those two years I learned nothing.

I have tried to open a breach in the heart of the young, but they have carnal drives not allowed to the old. A body that has given birth, that has known the unction of coitus, a body that has felt the murmur of life and that has become accustomed to the seed of man, cannot forget. Even if it lives on the Naviglio, algebraic sum of Italian consumerism, Brera renovated and dim. I watch the widows lean from their windows along the renovated dock with secret intentions other than the contemplation of people. In those waters of solitude many women have forcefully thrown the memory of a man they truly loved. Women who every day defy the pain so as to survive and who, like paradoxical assassins, are accused by their children.

I would have never thought that someday others would read about my suffering. And, while I write this, in the house on the Naviglio, I weep. Tears come like violent roe-bucks.

It is so difficult to live in Milano. After four years of being away I found a Milano undone by the thirst of progress. I no longer recognized myself in it. The South is warm and welcoming, always ready to lend a hand. In my view, the poverty so stressed in many books about the South does not exist. And, in addition, they believe in nature. Milano is cold and abusive, even if the city is a true empire. I was born here, but I have lived in misery, alienation, and was marginalized here in Milano. In the ward they call me *slut*, though I never betrayed my husband.

These two years of prison have no solution, neither in memory nor in song. Lost in the fog of a Milano abundant in love, I have no resting place, I have no love. No one loves me, and I am still not strong enough to know how these two years could leave a memory: that of a dazzling poet. I was lost in the fog of destiny. Why grasp at a pigeon that quietly rests on a branch?

Oh my mother, whose contorted lies made me into a corrupted victim of love and gave me death.

Oh my mother, every time they anointed me they touched your heart: the anointers of malice are like that. But the true voice that flooded the dawn, the song of my hidden innocence, was only your word. You were my word. Even my physical pain, you. Biting the apple of sin, they found me ready to defend you the way the body defends its breath. Mother, every time they treated me badly, they pushed you into the shadows.

How could I say that you were not spherical, though you were perfect! How could I have crossed your gulf, I your perfect light ship. How could I not confide in you, my love, while he betrayed me.

You were the world of the Madonna. Praying to you I prayed to her. And when they scratched my birth with a vision of evil, Mother, they wounded your indomitable breast.

My mother was like a tiger and protected even my children. Mother, I owe you this: the divine flame of my voice. Who dared offend you, proud lioness, by offending your daughter? You now live in virgin forests. You are the only far-seeing one.

But a young man, a sainted young man, one day, Mother, kissed my heart, there, where it bled heavily. A sainted young man without malice understood that I was not lying and that I had been critically wounded. This young man leaned over me, like the Magdalene with her long hair, and washed the great wound of my love that opened only for Christ. Through this one act of love I forgot the cruelty of my man, who had caused me so much suffering. This child too has been your child. He gathered up my poor flesh that had been cast in the Ripa and anointed it with saintly forgiveness. To this son, Mother, I dedicate your memory.

Your innocence has saved me. Only you could have touched me in the emptiness of my black sin without suffering from it.

Psychiatry transferred my illnesses into offerings for the sages, and editors put them into their wallets. But you wanted nothing. You kissed this wrinkled skin as if it were youthful skin. You are a memory of Orpheus. And because of this act of love, I hope you will become sainted beyond the confines of a lost Palestine.

Now that I cry from my love for him, I search him out and would like to ask him: "Teacher, when will my hour arrive?"

Yes, the Teacher has passed this way. You know, one of the madmen kept saying, "I am the Saviour." Poor child, only the mad call out to God anymore.

In Milano, R. the editor showed up; he said that he wanted to publish an anthology of my work. I did not want to receive him. I would spend hours on my bed, feverish, prey to the most tremendous pain, crying like a lost soul. I no longer washed. The unconscious memory of that banishment, the paradoxical shame of having been placed among the prostitutes of Taranto, clouded my mind. Luckily I had the good sense, with the help of my doctor, to turn to psychiatry. The story of this love, which should be so beautiful, is instead scurrilous. I would go mumbling along the Ripa with desire for a man. I became an object of derision. I thought of my piano that I had left in Taranto, and cried in despair. On that piano I played the most beautiful romantic songs for him. That same love, so large, sent me to the walls of Jericho.

If my lover were to come and see me today, he would find me in thought, painful and acrimonious thought about a person who appropriated my language. I will try not to be seen by him, because he would say, "Is this the devourer of men?" Since my lover drinks and does not understand my "depressions of genius" (as Aristotle would say), we do not get along.

When he finds some dirt on the floor he says "See what a useless woman she is!"

Damned be that encounter in which our affection changed and the rigid arguments of fear became guilt.

There are moments of effusion that are worth eternal thirst. Where to find God when love is lacking? But if a tree can grow at the level of scorched time, the deep willows of my internal agonies too can be born.

I do not know how to mention your name, nor how to damn you. Not after that encounter in which you quickly looked into the eyes of the gamble you had taken with love. Your impure thoughts turned on you. Malevolent betrayals of luck made me proud of the shadows. You dug into my face dunes of tears. Not even my knowledge could knock you to the edge.

Why did you hurt me? Why did you not play with my love like a ball of knowledge and coloured thought?

D amn you, who were never able to uderstand even the shadow of such strong power, and become a magnificent king! You, inside this superb fable, would have been on your own blue throne. You, the sublime one of the round table, who carried the Holy Grail through space! My poor dear love, torn by shadows and suspicion. What are you doing in the tormented waters? And when you begin to navigate toward me, when you acquiesce, obscure marvel of the season, you become fulfilled with visceral vigours. And you never give in to sleep, so that I can take up the creature which you hold deep in your loins.

O n a day of pure dementia I went to visit a priest who was not yet confirmed. He was beautiful. He looked like Saint Anthony of Padova. I said to him: "Father, I am in love," and he scolded me like a good mother.

"You know, Father," I continued, "I have come because I would like to bear a child."

The Father was beautiful, with a rosy flesh that made one think of paradise. Quoting one of my old poems, I said: "The loins are the strength of the soul." The word *loins* probably upset the Father's religious sense.

"My daughter," he said "do you really want a child?"

"Yes, with all my life."

"Then you shall. If you turn your thoughts to Saint Anna, who bore a child at the age of ninety, you will find consolation."

I wanted to intervene by saying that I had yet to find Saint Gioacchino, but I felt as if he was about to propose himself for the task.

I sat through a very long Mass that led me into a deep depression. I took communion and the host rubbed against my gums making a sinful noise. I felt as obvious and shameful as a thief. At the end, a deacon opened the door to the church and I went through it once more chaste and demented.

It was a clear body, forgetful and breathless. A body that knew no fear. It travelled along the shores of the Naviglio, alone, raven-like, with the hurried air of someone who wants to hide internal nakedness or a large evil hunchback. This body did not have a soul, it vaguely remembered having lost it down there, of having made a mistake. A terrible hole in its memory forced it to walk up and down the Naviglio, prey to the most absurd panic. It was a body made of soul. People did not recognize it, or if they did recognize it they did not care to pay attention to it. It would let out beastly yelps, or whinny like a colt locked up in some horrible stable. Adventurous people would reach out with a kick, others would spit at it.

But the body dreamed, and the more it dreamed the more it became rarefied. It spoke a strange, grey esperanto, absurdly mixing northern dialects and Dantean rhythms.

One day the body died, crushed by an eighteenth-century coach that suddenly emerged from the pages of a book. The eyes startled out of that emphatic head, like two magic sphincters. It was the end. The children of the Naviglio ran to have a look at it. The most beautiful girl among them, one that looked like a good fairy, said: "Oh well, it served no purpose anyway."

But, suddenly, an angel fell from the sky, looked at the body with a smile, gathered it up in its bosom, and told the children that the body had not been destined for those ignoble sidewalks, it was a body with an address, because, you see, it was awaited by a love.

My grocer looks at me with reverent respect, I know he loves me, that he admires my soul and my silence. At times, he invites me to laugh and I gladly oblige in such things, to please others. The other day a monk said to me: "How many beautiful things God has placed in your soul! Have you ever thought about it?"

I answered *no,* and that I was at ease and happy with such forgetting. I also told him that sanctity should not be stared at directly, or else it will melt, as in the little fable of Eros. Then the priest caressed my hand and said: "You are still a child." It's true, and I ran outside. But that priest didn't understand one thing, and that is that while looking at him I was thinking that he was a stupendous looking man, and that I wanted to smother him with kisses.

I have a clear and violent hunger, a desire for love veils my eyes. We are all violent because we are in chains.

It seems that the *Monaca di Monza* really existed. A little old lady of the Naviglio told me. She existed and she was crazy, so much so that she washed her sheets on the stone of Washers' Way while drinking wine. She said to me: "You don't know this, but I knew her well, she was a friend. And if you like young flesh you can go to little William, who played the part of 'crazy Egidio,' and he remembers her."

"Well, why not." I answered.

"You see, the *Monaca di Monza* was anything but beautiful. Small, stocky, she wandered around the pubs and swigged it back. Oh, sure she drank, and that's why she was walled-up alive: because of the *barbera*. You want proof?"

The old lady took me to Washers' Way and there she began to scream: "*Monaca*, come out!" From the window appeared an ugly face, good enough to scare children.

"Tell this woman what part you played in *The Betrothed*."

The other woman, sighing, answered: "A large part, yes, very large."

"What did I tell you?" the old woman said, and the *Monaca* left the little window and went in again.

That night I had to take a strong dose of Serenase, protected by un-whore-ish white sheets.

This morning at the Centre some man wanted to be admitted, and he was well. His wife was screaming: "But what the devil does my husband want? Why are they admitting him? He takes care of the children while I'm at work."

But the mad one was immovable (the power of madness!).

At which point the other nurses said: "But what does this guy want? He's crazy." And the social assistant slapped one.

"We'll report you," the two said.

Between reports and arguments the madman checked himself into the Niguarda, where he calmly smiles as he thinks of his wife finally defeated.

Once inside the asylum, everyone thinks they are free to eat from my plate and give me advice. They seriously tell me to be more parsimonious, and not to enjoy life.

When I can, I run to the nearest juke box and play twenty Celentano songs.

Then I find myself alone and thinking that my husband is dead, and at that point I could choke every bottle in every beer hall.

I've heard that Giuseppe Verdi lacked any epidermal sensation, and that almost every day he would let the barometer guide him, much as we depend on the horoscope. But I may be wrong: my memory is not very good.

In any case, in the middle of August I wear a coat. One time a lovely Viking succeeded in entering my swampy literary fortress and invited me to remove my coat. The Viking was beautiful. I, a mature and sleepy victim of sclerosis. But I did not want to take my coat off. After three months of constant courting I began to think that the young Viking might want to see me naked, and it did not displease me.

As soon as I had taken it off and was looking at him enraptured, the swift handed Viking grabbed the coat, running off in full strides and leaving me there in an erotic fiftyish rage, fucked over, unheard.

The love I feel for my psychiatrist has been bitterly fought. But there was a time during which my mind sang like a fire-bird. This bird, strangely, was trapped in a nest of magic beliefs by some ancestral smoke, by unbelievable chains of guilt. Today this bird no longer sings, and its wings, when it rustles about in my heart, tickle me with such intensity that I have to leave. My doctor calls it a "biological alarm." I call it a psychomotor disturbance. But I also call it coming voice, postulant vision, peevish vision, divine vision (now that I have become atheist from an excess of pain, and I find God bothersome and, at times, consider him obscene).

Dante is a madman, not otherwise qualified. He dresses in an elegant overcoat bought with continued efforts and exigencies straight from a *Centro* manuscript.

He has a hook nose, an internalized but extremely magnetic gaze. He goes about complaining that he carries with him the net of his drunkard father, but he is sober. They placed him in the madhouse, and little by little they are taking him out. He has tried to paint landscapes (that is, he has tried to dream) but then, strangely, he said: "I like the nurse's ass." And they locked him up.

It would seem that for mad people sex is prohibited, that it is some sort of pathogenic hallucination.

One day, tired of seeing him rejected, I kissed him on the lips and flashed a smile of complicity. Dante threw away his cigarette, raised me up and said: "How did you break such heavy chains with only a kiss?"

Running off I answered: "It can be done, it can be done, Dante."

Then, off in a corner, I cried for that mad time, now dead for reasons of love.

My young thirty-six-year-old love has another love. First, he said to me that I was tender but not experienced sexually. Then, last night, I found him in the arms of a beautiful adolescent with blue eyes. I right away understood why in bed he would call me "my beautiful adolescent." Since my reflexes are slow and I always appear to be drunk because of my nevrosis, I threatened him with a civil suit. The prostitutes of the area stared at me in horror, because I had a rose in my buttonhole, two fabulous pendants, and a very fine pair of shoes. What was not visible was my distorted brain.

The poor young girl screamed at me: "You are out of your mind!", and I gave her two slaps and said to her: "In the name of a frustrated maternity." The poor thing did not understand. I left indignant. Then I begged my friends to let me check into the Neuro center.

For the last two years I've heard my building manager and another neighbour, a labourer, get up at exactly six o'clock in order to get to work. Their doors slam violently on my writer's sleep, but the labourer has the strange and absurd belief that he is necessary to life and just can't hold off demonstrating it.

Intellectuals, in this society gone wrong, die of hunger, of heartbreak and tiredness. The plumber robs you of your paycheck because "he uses his hands." He uses them in all senses and even manhandles your rest. And since at seven the manager does the garbage cans, I have to get up, because I feel a duty to take him under my protection, and I forget that I am older and more tired and more necessary that he. But so it is, the presumption of the poor man is horribly destructive.

One day my pharmacist, alluding to my poetry in *Testamento*, said: "Do you regret the whip hand?"

Yes, it's true. One regrets violence as an act of love, and death too. I don't remember the whip hand of the women's song, but something hybrid had desecrated my loins, my memory. From there had started my illness and my obsession.

They think me noble, long for my art. Instead, I am one of them and the only nobility I allow myself is that of a long reinvigorating sleep. And, if we concede that death reinvigorates everyone, well then, there are days that I would like to die in order to sleep: that is when I go to the Centre where I find my psychiatrist who has acted out terrible racial discrimination regarding metal illness, arguing that G. has more need than I to be cured (I do not know of what: maybe of the great desire to idle about).

I can accept, as tired as I am, that a young boy take his place in the depths of the great phylosophy of life and become, in turn, a great judge of dementia, in the aid of the poor. Illness is the miserable capital of the poor, which one innocently offers to a doctor, saying in a mute language: in the name of this poverty, or misery that you might want to call it, in name of the faith I have in you, heal me. Above all, in the name of God, who wants us all equal and happy.

In my house there is an old and stale cadaver. Or it might only be inside my soul. A cadaver that I have been carrying inside for a long time. The cadaver of an old man who maybe one day sold me for the best offer. And, for someone as Catholic as I, they cannot lose. This cadaver used to move about, but it died before I could scream to him about my rancor at man's unnatural egoism; that a woman who loves should not be sold to anyone at any price, not even for a life. I cannot conceive of such a thing, I would like valid proof to show that it is not so. That he had really loved me, like I had loved him till the day that I heard them say that he was going to die.

I knew it, I had always known it from the first moment, but not like this. And if it was so, why had he married me? In order to give me a new irresistible pain? He had not understood that I could not have held up under the strain of yet another pain? Or was his love so blind? Oh, God, love must also be the objective force of life, our force. We must distinguish pain from love.

Every day I search for a thread of reason, but the thread does not exist, or else I have wound myself up in it. Some time ago, only two years ago, the thread existed, and it was a wonderful thing to unroll and undo that great ball of thread. And in unrolling it I would sing, like Leopardi's Silvia. But for a while now that ball has become a horror of strange multicoloured filaments. There is even a musical colour. I have tried to turn the ball into reason. I have tried to love, and in two we looked at the skein that remained unaltered, offended and hard like a cuttlefish bone.

The level of unconscious words, this sick pain, is the sense of his death. Damned, curse you, at one time you embraced me! For two years now I have been walking behind a naked coffin, and there is no luxury that could repay me for so much pain. The sentence motivated by the mafia, it's absurd tying your neck up in real life!

And you, who maybe now sleep while I am here writing of him, tell me: do you know songs of love? I have seen you ooze with joy in the company of young girls: bloodless as they are, in comparison to real pain. Only pain is the true passion.

Desperation can generate dementia and the impossibility of believing in the death of a man one loves. Desperation can undo the largest gulf of Italy. But since he is dead and others have plagiarized me, I invoke the fortunate and happy young who believe in love. He is dead and the bells ring in jubilation because his heart has been freed. He is dead, and there is no university that can say that I am crazy (I am alluding to the great critics who have pawned me off at the pawn shops). Yes, I am there, pawned off in order to pay some obscure debt: that of the present life. You might not believe me, but I have loved so much for you: the assessment of those who did not understand my love does not interest me. I loved only him, with an army of great loves.

I know very well that they are trying to drive me crazy. People know that I am exhausted, out of energy and strength. Or, at least, they know that I have little money, and so take advantage of the fact to ask me for more writing. But I am ill. The reactionism of which I was accused in Taranto began the day I understood that he was about to die. Far from allowing me to live through this human pain, they raged over me like horrendous rotters and carried my desperation to the extreme. Meanwhile, he was slipping away.

Do you know when I began to love him? When he said, with human charity: "Tell me about Him." It was then that I was overcome in astonishment, and my mouth embraced the word. At that moment I ceased to speak. At times, my tongue becomes consumed by the swelling of memories. How beautiful, and flowing like a sublime adagio, he was. His words, his rituals, his consummations of guilt. How beautiful this great man-child was. He was the temple of himself. He loved himself and he loved others: it is hard to separate the path. But he loved me too. He drank me every day from the cup of his words, like the nectar of the Romans.

Do you know why I never returned, my love? Because I was afraid, so afraid. Such a great fear that it froze my legs in that corrupt ward. Oh, my love, silent and present. You do not have a tomb in Taranto, you are buried in Milano with us. This book is my gift to you. It would seem deplorable to me to sell your name, but this book was also willed by God, who gave me the strength to survive. And, if no one comes to my rescue, I shall soon die.

Today my house is silent and empty. Everything is lacking, and above all the presence of God. He was taken from me down there, in the South, when with a sleight of hand I was separated from Him, thus destroying our ineffable union. What is lacking is the breath of a man, a man attentive to my grief and my tears of happiness. I have never thought of myself as mentally insane, more like a poor devil. Negative experience makes us confront ourselves, and the patience of Job remains exemplary.

I have no money, I have little life, but my heart whispers in that terrible voice of the women in the ward in Taranto, who said to me: "Do us justice, from Milano!"

When I went to Bergamo to collect a poetry prize, they gave me a beautiful silk rose as a gift. Since then, I have carried it pinned to my jacket, solemn, derisive, and provocative.

Someone politely pointed out that women who wear roses tacitly offer themselves. No one ever thought that for me that rose was worn in mourning. A heavy mourning, because after the Bergamo prize I never saw my husband again.

Yes, I offer myself to the highest bidder. Above all, I offer myself to panic, but since then I have carried that rose on my breast; its name is Michele, its name is Alda, its name is desecrated matrimony. Its name is shame. Its name is everything, except "flower." It is a stupid rose, useless like human suffering when one has to suffer at the hands of others and not out of one's own earthly will.

I have been ill for two years, exactly two years, and I have wanted it this way. Once more, I have closed the heavy temple of my life. I turned back immersing myself in an indecipherable unconscious. The unconscious is rich, like the bottom of the sea, filled with corals and sponges, full of sirens and dream figures. Full of carnivorous flowers. I have lived here for two years as when I was in the asylum. The asylum is a large sounding box where delirium becomes echo. At times, I lived in the asylum voluntarily. Other times, without knowing it.

As I have already said in my *Diary,* that which I write here is neither truthful nor probable, in as much as I am recounting the horrific in an idyllic manner. Maybe one day I will write the real diary, made up of atrocious thoughts, of monstruosities and from an unnatural desire for killing myself. The real diary is in my conscience and it is a very sad tombstone, one of the many tombstones that have buried my life. Someone said: "Those who have lived many times must die many times." A wonderful statement that summarizes the terrible concept of the enraged stupidity of man, who does not understand the guilt of others and tolerates only his own.

D reams often rise up and walk about on my head like an elf, a little elf that disturbs me but also entertains me. I've had so many dreams! Sometimes, I have seen a magic light shine in them; other times, they were dreams as heavy as stones placed at the center of my heart. But I accepted all these dreams: I like shapes and figures, whether they are from the unconscious or not. If they did originate in the uncoscious, I searched for their origin. In any case, they were stupendous dreams, full of colour, dreams that would say: "Come, get up! Life is beautiful. It's like nature tells us it is. It is always external to your anguish." With that, I would sit up in bed and the dreams would disappear. And the pure air of morning would rush in and my body was a beautiful statue, the statue of a warrior ready to fight and struggle for the day.

T he hospital is close to home. I go there every day. I go there to rid myself of guilt, as I would in front of a public confessional. What I find remarkable about these Centres is the public stoning. The absence of a Christ to absolve you becomes funny, so you go back home and doubt your faith.

There was a time when my husband had wanted to join the Foreign Legion. This would happen when, tired and exhausted, he wanted to be free of everything. But in the Foreign Legion at least one dies. Not here. Regardless of the fact that we are all abusive of our wicked victories, we all go on living. In other words, it is a Foreign Legion in reverse, but we too have our social rejects.

When the cart from the story of Pinocchio went by, the one carrying the children to Toytown, that greasy man, round like a ball, pulled up everyone who happened by just to get more people and make more money. This, in short, is the epopeia of psychiatric raids. Even so, if they too were to close their doors on me, I would die. But the empty self in there, and the one that I desperately search for, is the image of the offended God.

Yes, the "flowering girls" are a true image. And maybe you remember the times of Sappho: in everyone of us there is, upside down, an era. You suffered as Orpheus. You remember it. I know, maybe, in times past, you too descended into hell, and I can perceive this sentiment of death in your temples: they pulsate in vain for a journalism that will dictate filthy chronicles. In vain you love consumerism. Great poet of love, my letters are addressed to you because you have known him and still do, and you know his feelings of love. He is buried in you. He lives in your memory.

In the name of poverty many homicides are commited. Poverty is invasive and does unbelievable things. Poverty crawls under the sheets of others. One day a doctor said to me: "But why did you have four children?" I answered: "Because they turned out well, and I had time to waste."

"Lucky you, but then you handed them over to social services."

So I told him that he was right, and that I had had them in order to cheat the State. The doctor believed me and burned me to ashes with his gaze. I wanted to tell him that the State had plagiarized me and had not cured me, and that I had to sell myself to indecent people who had even speculated on my creative powers: he said nothing. Whenever I would take my children to the child welfare centre, so that I could go into the public insane asylum, they would not even cry: I had to do it because I was poor. So I would take them there.

I am afraid. But what is fear? It is love, it is poetry and everything that it eliminates and absorbs. Fear is everything that makes me absurdly abstract. When I say "He scares me," I mean to say that he coerced me with passion. And I don't know the reason why I use this term. It is a way like any other to exchange meanings between poetry and fear.

If my children had come to take me home one day, I would not have begun my long, tremendous stay at the Centre. At that moment, aside from the inhuman pain of a lost love, beyond the impossibility of returning to the home where I had lived and loved, there was only the way of return imposed by survival. The prudence of my doctor, who had saved me once before, came forward once again.

Coming up against the confused dialectic of these stars of psychiatry, one cannot but succumb to their discomfort, seeing how they solemnly preclude every road to liberty. And since the patient has no one to help out, she goes to receive her blows. Already guilty for having been unable to defend herself, to defend her love, she willingly receives the punches and coercions unable to understand (but they understand).

If Basaglia was misunderstood, it was only because his way of proceding did not pay off. I am not making any direct reference here, nor do I want to confirm what I do not know personally. I am not a doctor, but even if I were I understand that empty "pockets" are useless against the abuses of a mis-educated and above all badly applied culture. I have been a victim of it as well, I am still a victim of it and I might certainly be one in the future if no one comes to my aid. But I do not believe that in our contemporary society there is some element disposed to charity.

One must also consider that at times sick people suggest that they want to be able to caution themselves, and institutions are by no means necessary to achieve this miracle. Personally, I was the brunt of all sorts of accusations: that I had given syphillis to an already syphillitic patient, and that I had plagiarized younger writers. This causes me to think of Saint Theresa of Avila, and all the saints who suffered solemn pain and no pleasure. And no enjoyment for us either, sexual or amorous.

But, unexpectedly, today I heard the voice of God. Of that contradictory and heavy God who gives joy to the poor and ditches the rich. And to Him I appealed to heal and quiet forever the speech of poorly constructed peoples (psychiatrists, for example), and I beg the few friends I have left to keep me from disappearing into a hospital again.

The definition of mental illness does not properly reflect the afflicted person's unease with her environment. The mentally ill live immersed in a chaotic and incredible prescience, with energetic pulses that approach the primitive. The sentimental instance is confused with the sexual instance. The ill person is in no condition to give, but can only receive, affection with all the delirium that goes along with such isolation in an adult.

A choice of this type is in any case a choice, even if it's the result of earlier conditions. The ill person transfers to the exterior chaotic and false energies that can give way to illusions of power: thus, the mentally ill person who defines himself as Napoleon is born. This, for the reason that the mentally ill person's solution is an enormous transcendence of real values.

What a strange coincidence happened to me at a certain point. What an odd crisscrossing of ages. With whom should I talk about it? It's impossible to talk to myself. I don't listen to myself because I have so many things to do and in any case I don't feel clean enough for my soul. However, sometimes I have to make an effort or else I'll end up in a bad way. That infant that survives within my soul must finally grow up, or else the priests will laugh at me.

Everything in the Affori madhouse struck fear in me. The heavy silences. The hard, undecipherable chains that the stormy past of my youth tied to my ankles. If I did not have G.'s piteous hand, I would have died during the first year in that hell. Once, a neighbour came to see me. Particularly saddened by my plight, he placed a beautiful dress on my bed. I looked at the dress in astonishment.

"It's for your return to the world."

Stupified, I answered: "When I leave here I won't be going dancing!"

"Yes," he said, "yours will be a teenager's inaguration."

That poor man, a post-office worker, was a good prophet. He gave no thought at all to my poetry, but he really cared for me and had understood my husband's incredible mistake.

My feet were almost always bare, I was not used to shoes. I was so scared that, as soon as someone came near, I would get down from my cot and run off. I must have looked like a frightened beast. A little bird that went off beating its wings against the hermetically closed windows. Later, when I saw A. S.'s studio I quickly remembered those windows, but there one could breathe in life, colour, space. They looked like the windows of a Notre Dame where there lived an erroneous Quasimodo in love with the beautiful Esmeralda. Once freed I went to the Centre in Via Washington: there was nothing that could make one more ill to the stomach than that assistance center where the sick would sit in their chairs waiting for their medicine. It was, after all, a ghetto and the air was of beastly misery. Unfortunately, misery is destructive and I've always detested it. With all illnesses, cures are out of the question, unless money is no object; the insane asylum is, among other things, constructed for the poor.

The years that followed my release were happy. I had become beautiful: if nothing else the asylum had enacted as sort of hibernation on my body: I was still young, and my face was innocent. The sick person is innocent and the poor person is so poor that she becomes sensitized to the enchantment of nature.

My daughter was nine years old when, sitting beside me in our miserable little kitchen, and seeing me decline day after day, asked me: "Mother, what do you think of when you suffer?" Maybe it was this atrocious suffering that caused her to leave one day, and commit many errors in judgement herself. But what can one say to an impotent daugther, a sensitive child that watches her mother metamorphosize?

My illness made it impossible for me to take part in their education. This caused in them great distortions (with regards to their happiness). On the other hand, this is the diary of a mother who has loved all the children she encountered and who, when she sees them suffer, becomes a hyena. When she feels offended by them she becomes dramatic and coercive. And when she loses them in the most difficult times she renounces even God.

The *Diary of an Other* is the diary of this mother. If I can be allowed to make a comparison with *À la recherche du temps perdu* I would have to say that I have behind me an enormous quantity of *temps perdu*.

Lost time as far as my children are concerned, when they knew nothing about me nor I of them. And we loved each other in that way, in the margins. But my insides screamed for them every day. Terrible days, and with atrocious pains I gave birth to them. Not being able to speak to them I gave birth even to the children of others and since birth, at the moment of expulsion, is almost enjoyable, mine was called "avid desire for love." In fact, my uterus desired sperm: but only for procreation. In order to see a child's eyes that would look up at me with gratitude and innocence. My doctor is a mother, she understands these things, even if, mistaken, she would like to enter my second creation (the way I would like to enter her psychiatric values). But it's not as if psychiatry is inhumane. What is inhumane is the pain that promotes it.

I have one thing in common with my doctor: too many children. Maybe this is the reason we love each other so much. But while she looks after her own (the mad), mine have fled. The asylum became an excuse not to see me.

The youngest one even ran off in search of a mother that certainly wasn't me. I had already abandoned her, had lost her along the road of madness, and my baby did not forgive me.

But do you know what madness is? For me it has been a great, unconfessionable amorous langour. A langour so painful and spastic that it resembled the painful throes of birthing. Catatonic folly, stupefying, environmental, criminal, and blood-thirsty, like the adored myth of Clytomnestra. One time an arm of my martyrdom went up to Golgotha. I think that Jesus is inferior to me in both greatness and tolerance.

Writing is a serious thing: one should be serious in writing, just as one should live seriously. Maybe I did not say in my *Diary* that the first five years in the asylum were terrible. We had all been levelled to a certain dimension in which the individual no longer existed. Forgotten, locked in a hall, we passed our days doing nothing. One poor soul (I'll call her Madame Thénardier, like in *Les Misérables*) would do the shopping for us, a collective shopping, where she would cheat us. She was an avid shrew attached to her money, absolutely ignorant of our illness and hers. Dramatically taken by her madness, she would anxiously bring us our poor things and would hand them out to us with the unctuous manner of a mother that divides her children choosing among them their vices or merits.

This woman horrified me. She died in a little bed, holding an unknown sum of money tight to her chest.

The physical strain of the asylum then transformed itself into what should have been a great amorous perfection, capable of communicating with cosmic creatures. In that environment my conscience was troubled by a miserable and religious condition, and the concept of God was born.

Those who want to unearth some sort of perversion during the composition of their poetry are wrong. What should be teased out is that human and highly tragic fabric that has fatally distorted the course of an individual's history. And this is the historical tenor of my life and of all the deviant creatures that find their redemption in the word, if not a compensation at the level of dream-like and mysterious life of the unconscious.

Yesterday someone said to me: "Poets are dirty pigs." This is the same thing that Dr. F. meant when he said that, in the case of lust in thought, the head becomes one large organ of self-seduction. The place of a knowledgeable and mysterious masturbation.

They think I'm ignorant. They asserted that I was an idiot emeritus fatally aided by a biblical voice. I know that, even if self-taught, I am not a cutlured woman. I could never stand the sight of teachers in front of me: teachers assumed, as far as I was concerned, specifically the role-symbol of the woman as mother and I did not want to exist as a product of this concept. I have always searched within myself for the identity of a creature practially unborn on the ethical and generative plane of created flesh. I, therefore, approached the generation of myth under the illusion (and maybe this is where my folly lies) of being God's daughter.

And today, Sunday, I don't have a penny in my pocket. The things I suffered through for N.! As soon as he had my poor soul in his hands he destroyed it, the same way that everyone else has destroyed me.

Everyone scolds me about the Tavor pills that I take when the pain is just too unbearable. Why? As a final tragedy I can no longer convince myself to believe in God, and I am always undone by pain. Those poor women in Taranto said to me, "Don't forget us." I can no longer turn to my literary friends. I've practically lived in garbage for two years, unable to do the things I should have. The doctors who visited me could do nothing more than monitor the moral and physical state of my abandon. Some told me that I spent too much, but I don't know what I could have been spending. Maybe I am so crazy that I no longer understand, nor do I want to understand, anything. If it wasn't for the horrendous residence that weighed me down, maybe I would have coped better even with his death. But no one has ever really helped me. Everyone kept to themselves. Everyone judged me. No one showed pity, maybe not even you.

Maybe some pages of this modest book, savagely written, will decrete my end. I hope instead that the karma of my new editor will protect me from all such fallacy. People don't like it when one points out their defects. And of course I too have some awful ones. But maybe there is something that distinguishes the mentally ill from the sane: non awareness. As I've said elsewhere, he is the innocent. But not D'Annunzio's innocent: he is the innocent from the Testament. And they are the ones that pay for everyone else. So I invite all those who abuse us in the name of prestige, guaranteed at times with a degree and a pretentious little social worker's diploma, to come to terms with their own human nothingness. I too once hoped for that piece of paper that maybe one day would have structured me, but then poetry was born. Between the two, I don't know who to damn. All that is left is a tender body, maybe too tender, that no longer recalls, after so many years of criminality and bad taste, of having conceived of love during fragile nights, when the moon descended, as the only level of delirium.

I know that you too betray me. Who would not find within an ill person his own changing destiny? At times money is so foolish that it takes some sound victims and has them sing unhaltingly.

Oh God, forgive that obscure currency that people thirst after, and that then abandons them. At one time the noose was poetry: now, it is only a dollar.

In the epopeia of this general betrayal, that is the betrayal of poetry, there is your betrayal, which is nothing more than the persistent shadow of a dead Orpheus. Finally, but myths cannot die.

All my books are tied to my mental illness, almost always wanted by others to witness my damnation. And right now, I can only give myself over to God's will, because this sad chapter of my life did not close with my death but with the complete exoneration of the real values of day to day life. Good-hearted men and women have helped me. Others have overwhelmed me. A book was born from it. Maybe it will be the last, since I have found peace. I thank everyone. I even thank the boys on the

Naviglio, who saw a poet crazy with love and solitude run around in search of a phone from which to hear a voice she would hear no more, invoking divine justice for two years.

One day, a distant person said to me:"You will write another diary." Here, I am delivering it to her, and I ask for pity, as woman and as mother, reminding her that she has two children, and that to believe lies is bad, and mistrust of the love of two poets is, more than bad, blasphemy.

I publish this book because of hunger, not because I wanted to write it. I publish it because someone bluffed. Because I need money. Because great works have been dictated by a deep psychological and moral appetite. And corporeal too.

To go to the Centre every day is frightening. I put up with gossip, infamy, and shame. Shame, because it's an assistance center for the poor, and because as a poet I don't like promiscuity. But the poor attach themselves to anyone who stretches a hand out to them, to save themselves. They survive a thousand shipwrecks, violently grasping at their own desperation until they all die in the same mud. I have looked for a man who might save this hope of mine. I did not find him. I did not find him in time. I will fall into the void.

I call my doctor as witness, "Help me!" I called out to her, and she helped me. If a woman is worth her salt, she can subvert time and emotions. I call her to witness my pain, but I also tell her that psychiatry and letters have nothing in common. And that there are some poets so stupid that at times they want to die of love.

I did not tell you the truth because there is no truth, the same way that there is no law. Who is there? Another chimera, another dream, another unborn daughter, because ... (Maybe psychoanalysis could understand how a womb could generate infinite ghosts).

Oh dear friend, near and far, who lends an ear to memory and future, do you know the mystery of my life? I don't.

I wrote my first diary voluntarily. I have written this one, the second, because I had no one to speak to. (I know that I have no more friends.) And so, the blank page became my analyst.

A man will kill another man for money. Cain is not dead, and Abel continues to suffer. Here is my story. The diary ends here. I will certainly go crazy if nobody helps me. No, madness has already struck.

Afterword

by
Ambrogio Borsani

There are creatures that need the strongest fires to melt the gold deposits in their internal strata. In the process of this alchemy they come to pay an enormous price. Frightening burns mark them with wounds open to the pity and indifference of the world. Their burning lives become stranded in the deserts of love, go beyond the infinite worlds of literature and disappear in desperate traffic of arms with a few steps. Or they divide, becoming both the sacrificial body and the person who sacrifices it, and they run to deliver the torn ear to the unknowing prostitute. Or else, they lock themselves up in an asylum and go off to die at the edge of a forest on Christmas day, during a solitary walk in the snow.

In these cases, it becomes difficult to separate the phosphorescent trace of their existence from the living signature left in their art.

And so too, Alda Merini's human and poetic adventures seem braided, almost inextricably, for the continuous resonances that her life and poetry share. We know little of the "Milanese young girl" that Pier Paolo Pasolini speaks about in a 1954 article in *Paragone*. But, already in the poems collected under the title *The presence of Orpheus*, in 1953, one can detect the restlessness and thirst for the absolute that dominate the soul of their author.

"Not Rebora," says Pasolini, "but certainly Campana, from Romagna, not to mention the Germans, Rilke or George or Trakl, to mention a few: for reasons of racial proximity, for the analogies of *langue*, for the psychological substrate and pathological phenomena."

And it's odd to hear Pasolini mention Campana's name, years before Alda Merini's dramatic destiny took a turn in many aspects similar to that of the author of *Orphic Songs*. The young Milanese poet would publish three more collections (*Fear of God*, 1955; *Roman Wedding*, 1955; *You Are Peter*, 1961) before twenty years of illness ensued, ten of which were spent in an insane asylum.

Rising from the burrows with new, and incredible energies, she wrote *The Other Truth: Diary of an Other*, in which she narrates the memories of her underworld. It is her first book of prose. It is a scabrous and dramatic tale, a chronicle of torture and hallucinations in the clinics for the mentally ill. With *The Other Truth* Alda Merini seems to have paid the urgency of informing her readers about her long explorations within the continents of her illness. In this new book, *A Rage of Love*, having gone beyond the need for a report, Alda Merini once again takes up the material of *Diary of an Other* transforming the interiorized chronicle into lyric prose. In these pages, everything that is touched, even the most painful theme, is transformed into poetry. Every word is a key that finds organ pipes ready to amplify and sublimate the desperation. It's like finding one's self in front of a phenomenon of unconscious lyric power. "There is, in its movement toward us", writes Giovanni Raboni, in his introduction to the collection of poetry entitled *Testament*, "a velocity, a grasp of fluidity and almost impetuousness, as if something (a voice?) really were about to emerge from somewhere or someone: generously and unimpeded. I believe that in this regard it is possible, or, rather, a duty, to speak of a "gift," of an expressive and clamorously natural talent. Really a force of nature."

This is true, though it should not induce us to think of a Merini "possessed," of a Merini as instrument, a simple poetic medium. Of course, even parabolic antennae and television relay stations hide sophisticated and advanced instrumentations. And so, one must think of Alda Merini as a human structure with the gift of an exasperated sensibility that allows her to act on the page with a "savage impetuousness," as Giorgio Manganelli writes in his preface to *The Other Truth*. An instinctive and violent writing that, nevertheless, has nothing to do with primitiveness, for the care of word choices, for the bitter irony that is able to infiltrate even the most compact walls of pain through the bold leaps of the metaphors.

This *A Rage of Love* is divided into three parts. The separation does not take place in a net sense, but through the materials accumulated in the writings that circulate around three themes with branches and various subthemes.

The first circle represents a sort of self genesis, of poetry as well as the illness. The second contemplates the moment of a love lived at the limits of reason, and coincides with the period spent in the hell of the Taranto psychiatric centre. The third movement returns to the present, the daily life on the Naviglio and the dreams that this woman of extraordinary resources is still able to develop after immersions, drownings and rescues from the dark waters of the most cruel reality.

Those who know and have spent time with Alda Merini also know that every moment of her life is lived twice. First, in reality; then, in her fantastic projection. And it is here, in this cerebral celluloid, incisive, developed and projected on the magic screen of the page, that finally the author takes revenge on life.

The term "slow fire" recurs frequently in the books and dialogues of Alda Merini. And even if she often speaks of wanting to reject the bitter chalice of suffering, she is well aware of being a "slow fire," in other words, of being the point at which reality is ignited and burned, so that the metamorphosis may take place, transforming itself into incense.